Andrew Jackson's Presidency
Democracy in Action

Steve Wilson

PowerKiDS press™

New York

Published in 2017 by The Rosen Publishing Group, Inc.
29 East 21st Street, New York, NY 10010

Copyright © 2017 by The Rosen Publishing Group, Inc.

Book Design: Tanya Dellaccio

Photo Credits: Cover https://commons.wikimedia.org/wiki/File:Andrew_jackson_head.jpg; pp. 5, 8, 13, 14, 15, 17 Everett Historical/Shutterstock.com; p. 6 Elizabeth W. Kearley/Moment Mobile/Getty Images; p. 7 Interim Archives/ Archive Photos/Getty Images; p. 9 https://en.wikipedia.org/wiki/Andrew_Jackson#/media/File:Andrew-Jackson-disobeys-British-officer-1780.png; p. 10 Susanne Schafer/AP Images; p. 11 https://commons.wikimedia.org/wiki/File:Tennessee_Gentleman_portrait_of_Andrew_Jackson_by_Ralph_E._W._Earl.jpg; p. 18 Infomages/Shutterstock.com; p. 19 https://en.wikipedia.org/wiki/Bank_War#/media/File:General_Jackson_Slaying_the_Many_Headed_Monster.jpg; p. 20 Kean Collection/Archive Photos/Getty Images; p. 21 https://en.wikipedia.org/wiki/Trail_of_Tears#/media/File:Trail_of_tears_map_NPS.jpg.

Library of Congress Cataloging-in-Publication Data

Names: Wilson, Steve, 1943- author.
Title: Andrew Jackson's presidency : democracy in action / Steve Wilson.
Description: New York : PowerKids Press, 2016. | Series: Spotlight on
  American history | Includes index.
Identifiers: LCCN 2015048096 | ISBN 9781508149507 (pbk.) | ISBN 9781508149385 (library bound) | ISBN 9781508149170 (6 pack)
Subjects: LCSH: Jackson, Andrew, 1767-1845--Juvenile literature. |
  Presidents--United States--Biography--Juvenile literature. | United
  States--Politics and government--1829-1837--Juvenile literature.
Classification: LCC E382 .W76 2016 | DDC 973.5/6092--dc23
LC record available at http://lccn.loc.gov/2015048096

Manufactured in the United States of America

CPSIA Compliance Information: Batch #BS16PK: For further information contact Rosen Publishing, New York, New York at 1-800-237-9932.

CONTENTS

SHAPING THE PRESIDENCY

The American presidency has been shaped by each of the people who have held the position. From George Washington to today's president, each commander in chief has left a personal mark on the office. But Andrew Jackson didn't just shape the presidency. He **influenced** the idea of American democracy as a whole.

Andrew Jackson was elected president in 1828. He served two terms. While in office, he helped turn the Democratic Party into a successful and strong organization. His influence also helped the United States adopt a two-party political system, which is still used today. Under Jackson, the office of president became more powerful.

Jackson's presidency wasn't entirely good, though. His treatment of Native Americans was **tragic**. Thomas Jefferson once remarked that Jackson was "unfit" to be president. Whether Jackson's **legacy** is "good" or "bad" depends on whom you ask.

Andrew Jackson is one of the most studied presidents. The way he molded and shaped the presidency is an important part of American history.

A CHILD OF THE FRONTIER

Andrew Jackson was born on March 15, 1767. He was born in the Waxhaws region near the border of North Carolina and South Carolina. It was a rural **frontier** at the time.

Jackson's parents immigrated to the Carolinas from Ireland in 1765. His father died shortly before he was born. Jackson's mother raised Andrew and his two brothers, Hugh and Robert, alone.

This sign stands near Andrew Jackson's birthplace in South Carolina.

Andrew Jackson was a true child of the American frontier. As a boy, he often picked fights with other kids. He also taught them how to shoot guns, wrestle, race, and fish.

Jackson didn't have much schooling as a child. There weren't many opportunities to get a formal education in the backwoods of the Carolinas. Jackson was more often found playing pranks and getting in fights with boys in town. However, Jackson's mother wanted him to become a minister, so some education was necessary.

Jackson began attending school when he was around eight years old. However, fighting during the American Revolution soon arrived in the South. When it did, it interrupted Jackson's schooling.

A BOY IN BATTLE

The American Revolution greatly affected Jackson's life. His brother Hugh died in battle in 1779. In 1780, British forces defeated **militia** forces fighting near Waxhaw. Jackson, his mother, and his brother Robert helped care for wounded soldiers. A few months later, Jackson and Robert joined the militia themselves. Jackson was only 13.

Jackson served in the militia as an **orderly** and a

This political cartoon was created by Benjamin Franklin in 1754. It represents the American colonies as separate pieces of a snake. The cartoon says the colonies must unite or they will fail. This cartoon became a symbol of unity during the American Revolution.

As a boy, Jackson showed he was a fighter who stood up for his beliefs. This **reputation** *followed him to the White House.*

messenger. The brothers were captured in 1781 by British forces. In a story that has now become legend, a British officer ordered Jackson to clean his muddied boots. Jackson refused, and the officer swung his sword at him. Jackson had scars on his face and left hand for the rest of his life.

While prisoners of the British, the brothers became very sick with smallpox. Shortly after they were released, Robert died of the sickness. Jackson survived. While he recovered, his mother left to help with the war effort in Charleston, South Carolina. There, she died from a sickness called cholera. With no surviving family, Jackson became an orphan.

ENTERING POLITICS

After his mother's death, Jackson lived with his mother's family. When he was 17 years old, he decided to become a lawyer. He studied law in North Carolina. In 1788, he moved to present-day Tennessee. He became a successful lawyer in Nashville and soon had a thriving practice. This introduced him to people who were important to local politics. Soon, Jackson became involved in politics himself.

Andrew Jackson signed this document, which is now kept in the South Caroliniana Library in Columbia, South Carolina.

Tennessee became a state in 1796. Jackson was part of the group that wrote the state's constitution. He was elected the state's first representative in the House of Representatives and became a U.S. senator a year later. After leaving the Senate, Jackson stayed active in Tennessee's politics. In 1802, he became the major general of the state's militia. This positioned him to become an important leader in the War of 1812.

A WAR HERO

In 1812, the United States entered into a war with Great Britain. Jackson pledged the help of his militia to the U.S. government. In 1813, he was put in charge of fighting the Creek Indians, who supported the British. He successfully defeated the Creeks and earned a reputation as a powerful commander.

In 1814, British forces moved through the southern United States. Jackson followed them with his army, winning important battles in Mobile, Alabama, and Pensacola, Florida. Jackson learned the British were headed for New Orleans, and he prepared an army there.

Despite being inexperienced and outnumbered, Jackson's army defeated the British during the Battle of New Orleans. Jackson became a national hero and a legend. Soon, people began seeing Jackson not just as a military hero, but also as a potential president.

Jackson was known to be "as tough as hickory wood" on the battlefield. His troops gave him the nickname "Old Hickory," which stuck with Jackson throughout his presidency.

A HERO BECOMES PRESIDENT

Jackson first ran for president in 1824 against three other candidates. Jackson won the popular vote, which means he received the most citizens' votes. He also won the electoral vote. That means he had the most votes from the Electoral College, which is an organization that elects the president. Even though he had the most electoral votes, he didn't have the majority, or more than 50 percent, of them. Therefore,

In this illustration, newly elected Andrew Jackson greets supporters as he travels to his new home—the White House.

Jackson was sworn in as president on March 4, 1829. Here, Jackson is seen taking the oath of office, which is performed by Chief Justice John Marshall.

he didn't win the election outright. In cases such as this, the House of Representatives decides who becomes president.

Congress chose John Quincy Adams to be president in 1824. But Jackson had another chance four years later. Jackson campaigned as a man of the people. Coming from the American frontier, Jackson seemed to represent the common man. He promised to rid the government of **corrupt** politicians. He publicly went against the **aristocracy**. His reputation as a war hero helped him win a lot of votes, too. Jackson's campaign worked, and in 1828, he was elected the seventh president of the United States.

THE POWERFUL PRESIDENCY

Under Jackson's leadership, the office of president became stronger and more powerful. One way Jackson achieved this was by exercising his power to veto.

A veto is the right to **reject** a decision made by a lawmaking body. For example, the U.S. president has the right to reject bills that the House of Representatives or the Senate has passed. Andrew Jackson used his veto power more than any of the presidents who came before him. In fact, he rejected more bills than the six presidents before him combined! His willingness to veto made it clear that he would not let Congress boss him around.

Jackson also helped give more power to the central government. Once during his presidency, South Carolina refused to obey a federal law about taxes. Jackson issued the **Nullification** Proclamation, which said states did not always have the right to make their own decisions. Congress passed a bill that gave Jackson the power to send soldiers to South Carolina to enforce the law, but that wasn't necessary.

Some of the people who disliked Jackson felt that he took his power too seriously, and that he made decisions that only he wanted. They called him King Andrew I. This political cartoon shows Jackson as a king, standing on the Constitution.

CONSTITUTION
of the
UNITED STATES
of America

Virtue   Liberty and   Independence
Internal Improvements
U. S. Bank

TAKING DOWN THE BANK

One of the greatest accomplishments of Jackson's presidency was his veto against the Second Bank of the United States. Founded in 1816, this organization was a private business that controlled the government's financial matters, including **currency**, loans, and more.

To Jackson and his party, a central bank went against the idea of democracy because it benefited only the wealthy. In their opinion, the bank was a **monopoly** that had too much control over the American

Andrew Jackson's portrait has appeared on the $20 bill since 1928.

Jackson's veto against the bank showed Americans that he was willing to go up against the rich and powerful people in government. This cartoon shows Jackson, left, fighting states that supported the idea of a national bank. The states are depicted as a monster with many heads.

economy. They felt it went against the common man.

In 1832, a bill to keep the bank operating came before Jackson, and he vetoed it. The American people supported this decision, but it divided the American government. Because of this issue, two clear political parties emerged: Jackson's Democratic Republicans and the National Republicans, who were also called the Whigs. The effect was lasting. Today, the United States still follows a two-party system.

INDIAN POLICY

Jackson created an image of himself as a president of the people, but that didn't include all people. His treatment of Native Americans is considered a tragic part of his legacy.

In the 1800s, gold was found on Native American homelands in the southeastern United States. American settlers and people in government wanted these lands. However, Native American groups in

The Indian Removal Act affected the Chickasaws, Choctaws, Creeks, Seminoles, and Cherokees. All of these communities traditionally lived in the southeastern United States.

The Cherokee people were forced to march to Oklahoma and Arkansas using three routes, which are pictured here.

the region did not want to hand them over. The Supreme Court ruled that the lands rightfully belonged to the native groups. Still, many Americans demanded action.

Jackson didn't listen to this ruling. In 1830, he signed the Indian Removal Act. This act gave the president the power to **negotiate** treaties that forced Native Americans to give their land to the United States.

From 1838 to 1839, the U.S. military forced the Cherokee people from their home. They were forced to march to a **reservation** in Oklahoma without proper food, housing, or clothing. Many became sick, and about 4,000 people died. This time of terrible suffering is called the Trail of Tears.

A LASTING LEGACY

Jackson served two terms in office, for a total of eight years. When he left office in 1837, he was more popular than when he entered it. This is unusual for presidents.

Jackson's time in office had a lasting effect on how Americans view the presidency. Jackson appealed directly to voters. Many people viewed him as a common man, someone who was just like them. Many presidents after him have tried to do the same.

Jackson's actions as president also created a sense of what American democracy is. Under Jackson, democracy was portrayed as government that operated with the common people's best interests in mind. The presidency became more powerful under Jackson, and the Democratic Party was a successful and strong organization. These ideals continued to affect American politics for decades after he left office.

GLOSSARY

aristocracy (air-uh-STAH-kruh-see): The highest class in society.

corrupt (kuh-RUPT): Acting dishonestly.

currency (KUHR-uhn-see): Money.

frontier (fruhn-TEER): The border between wilderness and settled territory.

influence (IN-floo-uhnz): To have an effect on someone or something. Also, the effect of one thing on another.

legacy (LEH-guh-see): Something handed down over time.

militia (muh-LIH-shuh): A military force made of civilians.

monopoly (muh-NAH-puh-lee): One person or organization's total control over an industry or product.

negotiate (nuh-GOH-shee-ayt): To try to reach an agreement.

nullification (nuh-luh-fuh-KAY-shun): To make something have no use or value. In 1832, this term referred to South Carolina's refusal to obey a federal tax law.

orderly (OHR-der-lee): A soldier who carries out orders for an officer.

reject (rih-JEHKT): To refuse or turn down.

reputation (reh-pyoo-TAY-shun): The beliefs or opinions that are generally held about someone or something.

reservation (reh-zuhr-VAY-shun): Land set aside by the government for a Native American group or groups to live on.

tragic (TRAH-jihk): Extremely sad.

23

INDEX

PRIMARY SOURCE LIST

Cover: Portrait of Andrew Jackson. Created by Ralph Eleaser Whiteside Earl. Oil on canvas. 1835. Now kept in the White House, Washington, D.C.

Page 5: Portrait of Andrew Jackson. Created by Thomas Sully. Oil on canvas. 1845. Now kept in the Andrew W. Mellon Collection in the National Gallery of Art, Washington, D.C.

Page 11: *Tennessee Gentleman*. Created by Ralph Eleaser Whiteside Earl. Oil on canvas. ca. 1828–1833. Now kept at The Hermitage, Nashville, Tennessee.

Page 19: General Jackson slaying the many headed monster. Created by Henry R. Robinson. Lithograph. Created in 1833 and published in 1836. Now kept in the Anne S.K. Brown Military Collection at the Brown University Library, Providence, Rhode Island.

WEBSITES

Due to the changing nature of Internet links, PowerKids Press has developed an online list of websites related to the subject of this book. This site is updated regularly. Please use this link to access the list: www.powerkidslinks.com/soah/jack